| RECONCILED |

Black by Experience

My Struggle for Legitimacy

DANA CLARK-JACKSON

TOTAL
PUBLISHING
& MEDIA

ISBN: 978-1-63302-051-1

About the Author

D ana Clark-Jackson is a Life Skills Coach and owner of Life Solutions of Norman. She is happily married to Pastor Robert L. Jackson, proud mother of six and grandmother of seven and counting. A much sought-after speaker and educator, she holds a Masters in Human Relations and a Bachelors in African/African American Studies from the University of Oklahoma, and earned a certificate in Fine Arts from California Baptist University Riverside, California.

Born into dysfunction and rejection at a time when race relations were in the midst of upheaval and transition, she shares her story of redemption and triumph over prejudice and hatred through the power of love and forgiveness. A truly remarkable story....

To my wonderful husband;
Who has been by my side through every test and trial that dysfunction could bring; Thank you to my children who have paid the price so many times for the cost of ministry, and to my close friend Lynn Potts, my heartfelt thanks and deep appreciation cannot be measured in words, the Lord will reward every labor of love.... Thank you

Table of Contents

WHEN GRACE IS ENOUGH

T he definition of Grace is unmerited favor, it is the unearned and imputed righteousness of God; something that is unobtainable in one's own strength. This is my testimony and what has prompted me to share my story. My name is Dana Lynn Jackson, my maiden name is Clark, and I am the Great Great Great Granddaughter of Evangelist Maria Woodworth-Etter. I am a wife, a mother and a grandmother. I am a vocalist, a writer and counselor, but most of all, I am a recipient of God's wonderful and miraculous grace.

~ Me & Grandma Jesse ~

1959

Black by Experience

My skin-olive
My speech-sometimes slang
My walk – a high stepp'n swagger
Mellowed by education

But I am... Black by experience

My mother – a preacher's daughter gone astray
Left that thing called the white way
Found the other side of the tracks
Where the burdens are carried on broad shouldered backs

Making me... Black by experience

Hair – kinky/curled
High – cheek – boned
Native – round face
Not your norm

But still... Black by experience

Was poverty bound
But higher ground found me
Head stretched high
Heavens in sight
Broke free from tyranny
Ethnicity still intact

And yes, I am still... Black by experience

By: Dana Jackson, 2010

The aforementioned poem was written at the beginning of my graduate program while attending the University of Oklahoma, it culminated all that I had learned as an undergraduate African/African American Studies major and served as the personal launching point of self-discovery on multiple levels. To begin with, my birth was surrounded by controversy, from the negation of my father's name on the birth certificate, to the missing information concerning my racial make-up. The journey has been a long and eventful one, and no doubt will continue to be both arduous and enlightening along the way. A journey that serves a greater purpose than just finding my family roots, one that will no doubt aid greatly in the discovery of my ultimate destiny and purpose here on planet earth. With this in mind, I invite you into an intriguing look at what part race has played in my personal and life-long development.

PART I
Too Small to Understand

Chapter 1
Birth to Age Four

I am a long way from the sights and sounds of a young girl born to Middle America in 1958, nestled deeply within the city of Muncie, Indiana. The first five years of my life are still somehow distant, just a glimpse here and there: the scent of fresh ripe purple grapes draping over an old wooden archway in a neighboring backyard; the brilliant colors and memories of freshly picked red rhubarb growing wild that I could never seem to resist plucking on the way to kindergarten; and especially the huge encompassing cafeteria at Blaine Elementary where I could obtain endless glasses of water without being noticed, or so I thought. These are the little things I recall of my early childhood and the beginning of a life long struggle.

My recollection of the exact date and time of my mother's departure for California during the spring of 1963 is vague at best, she was forced to sneak away in the night in order to avoid my childhood cries of disapproval, or perhaps the fear of having a change of heart concerning her decision to leave would have prevented her departure. It was the same year that the bombing took place at the 16th Street Baptist Church in Birmingham Alabama It took place during the month of August.

I can remember a woman by the name of Ms. Hannah, who became my refuge and fortress from the unknown, the woman who wrapped a tight cocoon around my world and kept me safe. How ironic now that I look back, a caregiver with the biblical name Hannah. She had no children of her own - at least none that I can recall, yet she became my constant companion and guardian angel in a strange kind of way. I don't know what compelled her to step into the role of caregiver, but I am truly grateful.

Ms. Hannah was a rather large and stout black woman who, in my mother's absence, did her best to make me feel loved. Daily rituals and sights included morning cereal (cornflakes) with powdered milk; afternoons watching her do the laundry using an old beat up washing machine equipped with old style hand-operated wringer, and at days end, the long hot baths with the traditional cleaning between the toes. I even recall the song she sang diligently, *"this little piggy went to market, this little piggy stayed home, this little piggy had roast beef, and this little piggy had none, this little piggy went wee-wee-wee all the way home!"* Followed by her bedtime stories that caused me to drift peacefully off to sleep.

These images of those times in my life would form the bedrock of my existence in this world. I have no doubt she was a praying woman and sensed God's intended purpose and plan for my life. I personally believe she was assigned to watch over me and to keep me safe from a hostile world. She did it well; I had no idea what existed outside the safe haven she provided me.

I remember old cupboards filled with Argo starch used for daily ironing. I could never resist sneaking a taste on a regular basis, only to hear Ms. Hannah chide me about it not being for the purpose of human consumption, "It's not for food baby!" she would cry.

Muncie was a bustling city, home to approximately 60,000 residents, roughly 5000 of them were Black. Yet, there was a small farm town feel, one that loved basketball, home to the Indiana Hoosiers. Like towns and cities in the Midwest, Muncie had no tolerance for the mixing of the races. On the contrary; it was practically headquarters to the Ku Klux Klan, a racist organization created after the Civil War to oppress

Blacks during the era of Reconstruction which at one time ran everything.

My mother was only 18 when I was conceived. As a young church-going girl in 1958 you were considered an outcast and a floozy if you bore a child outside of wedlock. Being a Pentecostal preacher's daughter pregnant with the child of a Black man meant total social rejection by the Decent Whites in the community - the result-being ostracized and isolated at best. As for a Black man, who dared to be intimate with a White woman in KKK territory, well... that was an offense worthy of the noose.

I am sure that neither of my parents had given much thought about the social ramifications that would follow. Like most teens, their hormones were speaking much louder than their common sense. In fact, psychologists suggest the brain's frontal lobe (the critical thinking portion) does not reach full development until age twenty-four. My parents were about nineteen years old at the time and according to my mother, they were both cultural rebels of their day - enter God's grace and mercy.

As a child, my mother had been somewhat spoiled and for the most part lived a very sheltered life, yet she would often be involved in risky behavior. Living on the edge was her favorite thing to do, at least for a church going girl anyway. She started smoking at the tender age of 12 and was quite the flirt as I recall from her colorful stories. In our conversations during the last few years of her life, she shared how she had always felt as though she had been unfairly compared with her sister who, by stark contrast, was very obedient - the eldest of the five children. This seemed to have fueled a constant sense of inferiority and lack of confidence on her part as a young woman.

When we conversed about the subject, I sensed she felt as though she would never measure up to whatever expectations had been placed on her during childhood and this would in fact have a profound effect on our relationship as well. I believe it was a seed sown early into her life that would prove to be a catalyst for her future rebellion against so-called authority, however; nothing could have prepared her or my father for what they were about to encounter.

There would be numerous rumors and whispering at the local church concerning the preacher's daughter. The botched adoption plan followed by the bold step of bringing an illegitimate biracial child into the world, and into the "white only" congregation, for dedication by her father, the preacher. This would take place in front of, what she believed to be, a very unforgiving and hostile environment. It really did not matter whether or not her perceptions were accurate, most likely they were. Nevertheless, in her mind, they were valid and would affect her for the rest of her life.

Her father, the Senior Pastor of the local fellowship who had helped to start many churches for their Pentecostal denomination, was no doubt well respected. This was not the kind of attention that he wanted for either his family or his ministry. A Hollywood producer could not have come up with a better plot or storyline, only this was real, and I had the starring role. This was to be my formal introduction to the world and the beginning of my life as a dual-citizen.

I can only imagine what it must have been like for my Grandparents. They were fine upstanding people in the community and had been instrumental in helping to start many of the Four-square, denominational churches throughout the country. My grandfather had even attended Bible College in Enid Oklahoma for a time and the ministry prospered greatly from their work. Unfortunately, the very foundation of their faith would be shaken by the actions of their own daughter.

Surely, a thousand questions ran through their minds about why their daughter would do something like this, knowing their position in the community. Any parent, not to mention pastor, would have been completely caught off guard and unprepared for the shockwaves that must have rumbled through their congregation. In the 1950's, reputation was everything and theirs was being tried by fire.

I am not quite sure what prompted my mother to travel to the other side of the tracks where the coloreds lived (the name Blacks were referred to then). In any case, whether it was sheer stupidity or just plain guts, it is what she wanted to do, and so she did it. My father, from what I can tell of him, was a very intelligent young man; surely he would have known and understood the danger of messing around with a white girl? I am positive somebody warned him about breaking the law. You see, up until 1967 in the court case "Loving v/s the State of Virginia," it was illegal for Blacks and Whites to marry. If you were an interracial couple and wanted to be together, your only option would be to live together outside of wedlock. However, this one brave couple took on the court system and won.

It was a strange time in our history. Muncie, like so many other towns, was divided down the color line by railroad Tracks. Although Blacks and Whites had to live separately, In this small town with only one high school 'Muncie Central,' economics forced both to attend the same institution of learning. While the traditional "separate but not equal" white and colored drinking fountains and bathrooms did not exist, the attitude was ever present. The fact of the matter was, it was understood by the residents that there were lines which should not be crossed. Muncie's Black Community was concentrated in three locations during this time. Whitely, Cross Town—near the Black YMCA and Industry near the Ball Brothers factory. However; when it came time for the Bearcats to play ball, all would be present to root for their team.

Although it is unclear to me exactly how and when my parents met, their passions ran high and they found themselves involved just a little too deeply.

This resulted in a promiscuous relationship and lead to my conception taking place in the back seat of a car after just one encounter. Although lust was equally prevalent among both Blacks and Whites, stereotypes of Blacks being sexually aggressive were prevalent and propagated through films like DW Griffith "Birth of a Nation," in 1915. Oddly enough, to my knowledge, my mother never used any form of contraceptives - that I know of, yet she never had another child.

My mother successfully hid her pregnancy as long as possible by wearing Levi's and her brother's oversized shirts. But when it was revealed she was pregnant, her parents sent her to a teen pregnancy home. Her family relationship became strained as plans for an adoption were being examined without my mother's foreknowledge or consent.

This placed an even greater strain on the family and resulted in communications becoming almost non-existent for a time. As a result, my grandmother was traumatized and had to distance herself from my mother due to the hardness of my grandfather's heart.

When the time came for my mother to deliver, she gave birth at Wayne County Hospital; labor was quick. Afterwards, my mother motioned for the nurse to bring me to her bedside so she could look at me. The lengthy delay brought with it an uneasy suspicion. "Something didn't seem quite right," my mother recalled. So she began to scream. "Bring me my baby!" "BRING ME MY BABY RIGHT NOW!!!"

After a few moments, the nurse appeared with me in her arms wrapped in a newborn blanket supplied by the hospital; my mother's fears were relieved. Once she checked to make sure all ten toes and fingers were accounted for, she rested a little easier. However, later she would learn why it had taken the nurse so long to bring me to her. It turns out that plans had been made to adopt me out to my mother's older sister, who lived with her husband in Los Angeles. Most likely, the thinking on the part of my grandparents was that it would be better and far safer for me there, but when my mother got wind of it, she would have no part. The sentiments were, she gave birth to me and I belonged to her. And, I was her responsibility.

Not long after giving birth, my mother decided she would have me dedicated to the Lord. On a Sunday morning bright and early in front of her father's *all white congregation*, my mother brought me to the front of the church. She placed me in my grandfather's arms, looked him square in the eye and said, "*You Will*" dedicate this child to the Lord. Afterwards, she walked out of the church with her head held high and never returned to a house of worship again, and would never encourage me to do so either. This proved to be a rift between her and the family and served as point of contention. For years to come, it would be just me and my mother struggling to survive. We would never be close to her family and the tensions would never be addressed during her lifetime.

My mom and dad lived together on the outskirts of town in a small house. Among his other interests and talents, I found out my father was an avid music lover and had an extensive jazz collection. My mother told me he owned his own record store and for a short time was very successful. In high school, dad was well known for his basketball skills. Of course, being recognized by peers was important and like most young athletes, his desire was to obtain an athletic scholarship in hopes of gaining a promising career; of course this would become a distant dream. Economic hardship, racism, and familial obligations took their toll. His life, seemingly not much different from many Black male athletes of today, became just another "Dream Deferred" a poem about disillusion (Langston Hughes).

My aunt Barbara, on my father's side, told me stories of how she and my mother would stroll down the street holding one another's babies, "Just to mess with people's minds." During this time, my mother was jailed for dating a Black man and made to wear a sign around her neck that read, *"NIGER LOVER!"* It is unclear to me when the trouble with the police actually took place but, according to my mother she was humiliated by the arrest and her stay in jail. With no real support system in place and the stigma of being tainted by involvement in an interracial relationship, my parents were faced with some very difficult decisions to make.

My mother would soon learn that my father was contemplating returning to his former relationship because of the potential income to be gained from a settlement. He was a married man, who according to him, had been forced to marry because of a pregnancy. This would plague their already fragile relationship. Their resolve would be thoroughly tested and although he and my mother were determined to be a family no matter what, they would soon find out that the social issues of their day were way beyond their control or ability to handle alone.

They were not alone in this, as there were also other children to consider; there were the four little boys, all children of his absent wife, and myself. We all lived with my parents in that small house directly across the street from my disapproving paternal grandmother. The full details surrounding how this came to be are unknown to me, but their lives would be affected as well. According to my mother, the four boys had lovingly referred to her as Earlene-Mommy and we all called my father, Jimmy-Daddy.

1962

The pressures of life began to take a toll on my parents. A conversation overheard by my mother, between the mother of the boys and my dad would prompt an argument that proved to land the final blow to their relationship. This forced the already tattered unit to be ripped apart leaving my brothers screaming and crying, "Please! Earlene-mommy, don't leave us! Don't take Dana away!"

The fact that Muncie's Black community had only one Pentecostal Church at the time - which no doubt my grandmother played for at some point, was indicative of the great divide which existed even among the faith community. I am sure it had to have caused a big stir among the locals and gave my parents a notable reputation. Disgruntled and tired of the racism, my mother chose to go to great lengths to get away from all of the pain and rejection she experienced there. She chose to move as far away from Muncie as she could get, traveling all the way to Los Angeles, California, leaving me behind.

Not long after arriving on the club scene In Los Angeles and having become a regular at the bars, my mother was awakened by a dream that seemed so real she broke out in a cold sweat. It depicted me crying out "Mommy-Mommy. Where are you?" this disturbing image prompting her to return to Indiana, where she had left me in the care of Ms. Hannah, and to take me with her, back to California. I can't say I was heartbroken about the move because there had been no real connection or friendships established in my life in Indiana. Other than loving Ms. Hannah, I was too young to have formed any lasting social connections.

Chapter 2
Life in California

U pon my arrival to sunny California, I felt like a mental tornado had torn through my young life. The first few years were just a blur. I had no real understanding about the tumultuous times we were living in; that would become self-evident in the very near future. The Civil Rights Act of 1964, the Selma Riots and the Right to Vote of 1965 were all taking place during this time. Even though we found ourselves right in the middle of the South Los Angeles Riots of 1966, I had no idea concerning the significance of what was happening around us.

My mom told me she had been threatened by the National Guard and told, *"If you set foot outside of your apartment complex, you will be shot!"* The National Guard was patrolling the area, **"It was crazy!!!"** The racial riots would mark a very crucial time in this country's history and these things would have a profound impact on my life. Even though I would not face the full effect until years later, I knew that something very profound was taking place.

Chapter 3
Life of a Chameleon

The move from Muncie and subsequent moves throughout Southern California afforded me exposure to many cultural experiences. Seal Beach was a military community, one that was small in number and predominately Caucasian. Even though I had not developed much in the way of having a racial or ethnic identity, I readily adopted the culture of those around Me: their clothing, musical tastes, likes and dislikes. This would happen throughout my early life and with every move came another adjustment to what ever environment that I found myself in.

The move to the inner city brought yet another cultural experience; instead of the sights and sounds of the suburban beach community with its relaxed atmosphere and laid back casual attire. I found myself in the midst of the African American urban community filled with smell of BBQ, Straightening combs and of freshly pressed hair. The music was different as well and stirred up a kind of restlessness deep down on the inside known for its distinct and unique use of polyrhythms.

Each move brought not only an awareness of cultural and ethnic differences, but also the understanding that I really did not belong to any one group or community. There was this feeling of never quite belonging, yet an ability to identify with all of humanity in the broadest sense. Sometimes it felt like an otherworldly experience-almost out of body but, essentially I just learned how to fit in wherever I could. It was like I was a kind of social experiment, I would soak up what ever came my way.

PART II
Self-Discovery

I can remember bits and pieces of the late 1960's, kind-of-like a jigsaw puzzle; chicken pox and tom boy wounds, roller skates, sting-ray bicycles with banana seats and most of all the discovery of boys. My mom seemed to do a good job in raising me as a single parent, at least as far as I was concerned. She sheltered me for the most part, as much as possible from the harmful onslaught of prejudice. She made sure I was exposed to the African American population by living in the community with them. Which must have been difficult for her at times, because I am sure prejudice ran both ways. Black women often accused her of stealing their men, as if there were tags around their necks that read for Black women only.

The world was hostile towards a White woman with a mixed child, but I never knew about it because she never discussed her hardships with me. She seemed very lonely at times and depressed, but she managed to mask it well. Children rarely understand the plight of their parents, for the most part they keep things to themselves in order to protect them. Over time I would discover the whole truth.

After years of moving from place to place, we finally found somewhere we could call home. Our first real stay would be on Harvard Blvd. located in the Metro area of Los Angeles; it was a very diverse community which was home to a multitude of ethnic groups. Nevertheless, there were mixed emotions concerning biracial children, especially in the White community where it appeared to be resented the most. I would learn about it in depth later on in life.

The Black community was altogether different; it was somewhat strange to see how highly prized a light skinned child seemed to be in contrast to the darker persuasion. We had the "good hair, the light eyes."- Something that was prized and to be envied. I would later learn the reason behind this social dynamic and would both come to understand and share that experience with others. I gained a great deal of insight while completing my degree program and coursework obtained in African/African American Studies.

Early years of my mother's life were filled with night clubs, card games, and time spent at her friend's houses drinking and smoking. She was a single mother, as such, she had to take me everywhere with her. Often this resulted in being taken to inappropriate places for a child of my age. Once I recall a trip to a bar and being allowed to dance in the booth where the Go-Go Dancers performed. This also meant spending many evenings without supervision, something conducive to healthy parenting. On occasion, after party nights, she would wake me during the wee hours of the morning and have me dance for her friends in the living room.

I was a ham and loved the attention. Everyone would applaud, making her feel as though she belonged to the larger community.

There were many instances of drunkenness that followed, more than I can possibly relay, but one night in particular comes to mind for me. It was very late and I was sound asleep when I was awakened by my mother's cries at the front door. I could hear her keys slamming against the metal as she tried unsuccessfully to find the keyhole.

She was sloppy drunk. She moaned and groaned as if she was in pain and her words were extremely slurred, but loud. "Dana! Open the door!" she bellowed. As I opened the door, I found my mother with clothes disheveled and black mascara stains running down her cheeks from the tears that had dried. I helped her to the couch where she plopped down and continued to sob over not being able to remove her boots. They were patent-leather boots and were stuck to her very white-stocking-less legs. These scenes were played out so often they all kind of ran together in my mind.

She relished acceptance by the Black community, yet her personal life was unstable and her emotional health was in an upheaval. She had become an alcoholic in order to deal with her pain and was dating one man after another searching for love and acceptance. This, of course, never produced a healthy relationship as most of them were found in bars; not a good place to find any type of stability.

Out of all the men who would visit us, one in particular stood out. He came by the apartment pretty regularly and was quite a gentleman as I recall. His name was Ernest Lane; I remembered him most because of his processed hair (a term deemed as such due to the process by which it took to straighten Black hair with chemical relaxers). It reminded me of my father's hair, he had always worn a do-rag in order to keep his relaxed hair in place. What I recall most about him was the fact that he could never pronounce the word pretty. He would say to my mother, when he looked at me, *"what a puddy guh!"* (pretty girl)

It turns out he was the real reason for her move to California. She had met him back in Indiana while he and the group he was touring with traveled through the Midwest. Ernest Lane was a musician who she had fallen for after meeting him at a club.

He was the keyboard player for Ike and Tina Turner's Review, an up and coming musical group; one growing in popularity. She had followed him and the group to California over the summer and would make California her home as a result. Unfortunately, I learned of his passing in October of 2012. It was also at that time, after reading his obituary, I discovered what a truly phenomenal musician he was. Of the many men in and out of her life, he was certainly one of the most memorable.

As I look back, I can see how music had a really profound effect on my parents. It would have the same effect on my life, both good and bad. My experience and appreciation for music would become very diverse as we moved into different communities and interacted with different cultures. I learned to understand social constructs, value systems, and even fashion by venue. I became familiar with Folk, Country & Western, R&B, Jazz, and so many others. During the early years, I would listen to whatever my mother would play on the stereo; for the most part it was the Blues.

I remember living in a small neighborhood across the street from my childhood friends and play cousins (a Black tradition and residual of slavery). This helped to establish an extended network of family and needed support, and made life for me more palatable and stable. Rolonda and Anthony McIntosh, who were also biracial, were stabilizers in my chaotic world and would become very close confidants during the next few years. Our mothers were drinking buddies and we spent a lot of time together. We went to school together, and played in the yard after school almost every day; we almost felt like a normal family.

Occasionally, we would stop by the Japanese owned neighborhood storefront grocer to get pickled pig's feet and dried-salted plums which were very sour to the taste. It didn't matter that we were not brought up to understand the significance of cultural diversity; we were just kids learning about the world around us and enjoying snacks. The economy was very different then, in the early to mid-1960's candy bars were only a nickel and they sold shoe-stringed licorice a mile long for three cents a piece.

One year, both our families had gotten German-shepherd puppies from the same litter, Ant-se and Woo-de (nicknames for Anthony and Rolonda), picked the male and I took the female. We named them King and Queenie; I personally believe the dogs helped our two families cope with the stress. They helped to provide a sense of normalcy in our sometimes confused world.

Our parents frequently went out to the clubs together, and would sometimes Leave us with baby sitters. Unfortunately.

On two occasions we experienced molestation and kept quiet because we were too scared to talk about it. The first instance was with a male baby sitter who was an older teen. After putting us to bed, and believing we were asleep, he slipped into the bed and pulled down our pants. We were both scared to death and faked rolling around in our sleep. He quickly got up...the coward. Unfortunately, these things happen more often than parents think, especially in today's society.

A second instance took place at a home which my mother had taken me to. She left me alone in the care of people I barely knew, so she could go out with her friends and have a good time. I was placed on the sofa to sleep. But once the lights were out, a man came into the room, pulled down my underwear and put Vaseline on me. I was so scared that I just froze. He was scared off when someone opened a nearby door. I was traumatized a second time, but never mentioned it to my mother because of fear, like so many other children who feel ashamed for things outside of their control. I believe until this day this instance provided an open door for the enemy of my soul and fertile soil to later develop a promiscuous lifestyle.

We lived there for two years when we had to abruptly move from the little house in the middle of the block.

Something happened, unknown to me. Whatever it was resulted in us having to move in with another family.

The second school I can recall attending in California was located in a small community by the name of Seal Beach. At the time we were there, I wasn't aware of any Blacks residing in the near vicinity. The beach was within walking distance from the house we shared with my mother's friend. She was a White woman who dated Black men as well, and who had six daughters, four of which lived with her. All together there were seven females living in the same house, I was of course the youngest and the only one of biracial heritage. Their father (a White male) had been away in the military in Thailand or India and had decided to stay there.

I never really understood the whole story, but they were kind enough to allow us to stay with them. They had a swimming pool in the backyard with a slide; and a dog named Savage, who loved to go swimming in it. Although we had brought Queenie with us as a young pup, there must have been an issue with the two dogs. One afternoon, after coming home, I realized Queenie was gone. There was no warning and/or sorrow concerning the call made to have her removed. It was done and no apologies were given. I was crushed. It wasn't long after that, we had relocated yet again. I don't believe we lasted a year there.

Me & Mom

(1966)

This time it was Los Angeles somewhere in South Central. I remember it well because we found ourselves right in the middle of the LA Riots. My mom told me it was so hostile when the riots broke out, that the only thing that saved her from a beat down by the Blacks was the sign she wore around her neck that read *"I BELONG TO A BROTHER!"* Somehow by the grace of God we were able to survive.

Over the years, I attended at least three more elementary schools in Los Angeles. My mother moved quite a bit which resulted in me having a real sense of insecurity. It was about this time I learned the school had a program called religious release. the program allowed for midday instruction in the Bible. For me it meant an excuse to get out of doing school work; I attended the services on a weekly basis. We would get out of school during the midpoint of the day and walk across the street for a time of Bible study. I truly believe it was at that time a seed was sown into my life about the Savior's love for me. I thank God for the little

Baptist church across the street from my school. It wasn't long afterwards the policy was changed concerning religion and the use of Bibles in the public school system. As for the proponents of the measure, I would offer up the present condition of our educational system as a reminder of the need for God's word in the lives of our children.

It would be in elementary school where I would experience my first crush, the L.A. Stomp (a popular dance) and the Jackson Five. Like all young Black girls, I was in love with Michael Jackson, the youngest member of the pop group, *The Jackson Five. I even* got the chance to speak with him on the phone once while in the 6th grade. Over the next few years, we would move frequently and each time I learned more and more about how to adapt to change, you could say that I became an expert at being a social chameleon.

Life in California was varied and location was everything; Central Los Angeles, Watts, Inglewood, and West Los Angeles. All were called home at one time or another - just to name a few...even Culver City was home for a few years during jr. high school. These were the most formative years of my life. Ironically, my fondest memories were during a three year stay at an apartment complex located near the Wilshire district of Los Angeles. That's when I lived on Harvard Blvd. and attended Hobart Elementary School. This place was home to me from the fourth grade until the sixth grade.

It was there, in the midst of the most diverse neighborhood in the nation, where I felt most welcomed and at home. We were even interviewed by the local news one year and had a spot on evening television which touted as the most diverse school in the nation at the time. It felt good to be noticed for being part of something positive. I was safe here and felt really connected to others for the first time in my young life.

Chapter 4
Grade School and Musical Influences

1970

I Found Music

S elf-discovery is of great importance for pre-teens. In the sixth grade I realized that I could really sing; this prompted me to join the sixth grade choir at school. I fell in love with music in the general sense, but pop music really caught my attention. Its influence on my life would prove to be very profound. I began to ask my mother for money to buy 45' records by a few of the popular groups of the time. The Jackson Five were all the rage and I was hooked from the moment I heard them.

I would dance around the apartment and sing the popular songs of the day. Artist such as the Osmond's, Stevie Wonder and the Supremes, but most of all I enjoyed hanging out with our next door neighbor who was a piano man. Earl Williams was his name; he and his wife Lois lived literally five steps away from our front door. I was a welcomed guest in their home at any time. I would hang out at their apartment when the musicians would come over and have a jam session, it was great.

Lois, his wife, volunteered to do my hair because my mother didn't have a clue about what to do with Black folk's hair. Being I was biracial, the texture of my hair was different than what she was accustomed to working with. Either that or she just had a strong dislike for mine in particular. I can vividly recall her raking that small toothed comb through my hair like she was raking a yard full of leaves and angry she had to do it in the first place. It didn't help much that I was tender-headed (a condition known and understood in the Black community as an inability to take the pain of a stern combing to the scalp.) Hair would remain an issue for me for many years to come, as my mother knew little about its care.

Friendships

Every child needs to have the security of having a best friend, and Carrie Ann Lew was my closest and most trusted friend. We did everything together, she was Asian and biracial as well, only she was Chinese and Japanese, so no one ever made a big deal about it. You can imagine what a joy it was when she recently found me again after over twenty-five years of separation. Her mother's friend, a police officer looked me up using the police data base and we were reunited. It was as if time had stood still for us. And no, I did not have a record on file.

We met my first year on Harvard Blvd. shortly after my mother and I moved into the two story apartments down the street. One day after school, she was being teased by some of the neighborhood children about having a metal hook at the end of her arm instead of a hand. This was due to a birth defect, yet she never let it stop her from excelling in school.

After I came to her defense, we became fast friends and were inseparable from that day forward. Then there was Roberto Villar, the third part of our three-fold cord. He was the cutest boy on the block-at least that was the general consensus. I believe he was from Venezuela or some other Latin country. He had dark brown skin with a reddish undertone, beautiful curly black locks of hair and a silver tooth, which just screamed heartthrob to all the females in the immediate area.

Carrie Ann was extremely bright and artistic. On occasion, I would attend Japanese school with her after regular school. As I look back, I realize her mother was making sure she never forgot her cultural heritage; it was a wonderful experience and I even learned how to greet the teacher in Japanese. Roberto was the athletic one, always playing tackle football in the front yard of their apartment complex. Then there was me.

I was busy, very busy, maybe even ADHD busy. But no one I knew had even heard of it as a diagnosis. I was always getting into trouble with the teacher; I could never be still for long and talked insatiably. I climbed trees with the boys, jumped rope, played tetherball with the girls and leaped across a roof or two. However; I would have to say my favorite thing to do was to ride my bike. It came complete with stingray handlebars and a banana seat. Of the three of us, I was the musical one. We were best buds; but again it would be short lived as moving was a way of life for me and my mother.

Dealing with Mom's Side of the family

Ever so often we would be invited to the family gatherings, and perhaps there were more than I was made aware of. My mother never put much emphasis on family gatherings nor did they seem to be something high on her list of priorities. However, the ones we did attend were always filled with tension. Although the discomfort may have been somewhat masked, it was always lurking right beneath the surface, both very real and unpleasant. There were the traditional holidays like Christmas and Easter. I never felt connected to her family and even now I am not sure if it was because of her doing or their wishes.

There were remarks about my complexion and hair texture made to my cousin. The absence of pictures in family albums were constant reminders of the disconnection. Phone calls were rare and time spent with my grandparents was nonexistent. There would be those awkward moments of Black dolls for Christmas and the birthday cards depicting people with darker complexions in an attempt to make me feel better about not looking like everyone else in the family. It was a reminder they saw me different from themselves.

It was always uncomfortable and we never stayed very long. Perhaps it was due in part to my mother's lifestyle. After all they were believers and had been church-goers all of their lives and she did not attend church at all. I was the elephant in the room no one wanted to talk about, but was a family member just the same. I guess for me the big question was, "where was Christ represented?" Needless to say, I had a lot in my life to process: who they were to me, who I was to them and who I really wanted to be in this world.

Chapter 5
Junior High, Gender, & Race

I was just finishing my sixth grade year when we relocated to Culver City. In 1971, I would get my first lesson about how very different a person who was racially mixed was treated by the dominant culture. It was in Jr. High School during the onset of puberty when it became apparent I was not accepted by Whites. It was here where socializing skills became a detriment for me. What happens when you are attracted to boys, but no one wants to even acknowledge you exist let alone you might be considered attractive.

There weren't many racially mixed teens at my school, but of the three of us, I was the only one that didn't quite fit in. It seemed to be understood since we were all mixed, we would eventually get together - no pressure there. It was me, another female, and a male. I was not attracted to him, I preferred Ricky Landy, the blonde haired blue-eyed 7th grader all the other girls thought was cute. I didn't think it mattered much about the color of your skin just as long as you assimilated into the dominant culture. After all, there were Native Americans, Hispanics, and even two other Black and White mixed kids, all of which acted like everyone else. That was not an option for me though; I was determined to be me, whatever me was to be. At least at this particular school there was a commonality they all possessed, it was called money. That and the fact that most came from a two parent home.

Culver City was the movie mecca of the world at that time. All of the major studios were nestled together within a five mile radius. I would often walk the back lots of MGM Studios and fantasize about becoming a great movie star. At the age of sixteen, I got the chance to visit David Soul's dressing room while they filmed Starsky and Hutch, a TV program about two young cops. It was filmed on location near my home on Venice Blvd.

I soon realized I was considered taboo and no White male in his right mind would ever date a Black girl or even look her way for fear of rejection from his peers. Considering there were no other choices available, I was just out of luck socializing on that level. The name calling ensued shortly after I took my mental stance against assimilation. *Flop-top* (a depiction of my bouncing afro-puff hair style) *Zigga-boo, Jungle Bunny, and the infamous "N" word* were hurled at me on a regular basis; ironically it came, for the most part, from the male students. The girls were much more subtle and whispered beneath their breath; after all they were lady-like. Their assault came across more in the form of a sniper attack.

1972

I still enjoyed outings with other young people like ice skating, the beach and backyard parties, but it was evident that I was the outcast. I would only make it through a year and a half of Junior High before my mother would once again uproot us. This time we moved to West Los Angeles, near the Laderra Heights/ Windsor Hills neighborhoods. Slauson and Overhill were the main cross streets and I walked everywhere. I walked to the parks, around the neighborhood and made a stop at *"The Witchstand,"* the restaurant my mom managed where I could get a free meal. It was a daily pit stop for me and once filled with food for fuel, I'd be on my way.

The Color Line

School integration was in full affect and forced busing had just become policy in the area we relocated to. So, an hour before school began at Orville Wright Jr. High, busloads of mostly Blacks and other minority students were trekked across town to a predominately all-White school in the city of Westchester. So now, instead of the hip-hugger bell bottoms worn in Culver City and the failed relaxer, which left my hair frizzy and broken-off at the ends - while trying to straighten it in order to look more like the White girls, I was faced with full-on afros, kids sportin' Black power fist combs in the back of their heads, converse tennis shoes and rolled-up cuffed levy jeans. I am now officially in full-on identity crisis mode! Who am I? What am I? And most of all, can I survive this transition?

I was halfway through my Jr. High experience and just now discovering a major difference in my culturally divided world. Since I was an only child, it was difficult to find a sounding board through which to filter my thought processes. I found solace in friends like Monique and Michelle Robinson, who lived off of Slauson Blvd, and who I thought looked like me and Joel Jones and his family over on LA Sierra Blvd.

31

In spite of that, living with just one parent, the White one-at that, never really fully provided me with an understanding of why it was such a big deal, this thing called the color line.

I was quite naïve to the whole thing but, my education was about to start. I took an interest in gymnastics after visiting the YMCA in Westchester. I was invited by a girl from Wright Jr. High, but there were no Blacks involved so I lost interest. When I was 14, my mom began working nights as a bartender instead of waitressing at the restaurant side of the *Which Stand.* This would leave an open door for all kinds of mischievous behavior. This is probably why she took the management position.

I went to house parties in basements, garages and any other place that looked inviting. I met all kinds of characters and tried a little bit of everything. I was extremely wild compared to other teens in my day- and then some. My mode of transportation was walking until my mother bought me a ten speed bike for my 15th Birthday. This afforded me the opportunity to broaden my horizons and to get into more precarious situations. Honestly, I don't know how my mother made it through some of the trials that I put her through.

Music was still at the forefront of my plans and I soon learned the background singers for Ike and Tina Turner rehearsed near our apartment. After school, I would sometimes stop by and join in on the dance rehearsals. They would encourage me by telling me what a good dancer I was, that I had a lot of potential and would make a great Ikette one day. This was a different kind of seed sown into my life; one of affirmation and positive reinforcement, something I desperately needed as my mother was never big on compliments. By the time that 9th and 10th grades rolled around, I had been fully immersed in Black culture, along with the Afro, black slang and the communal way of life which seemed to come so naturally. As usual my mother felt the need to find greener pastures and moved into Inglewood. More likely than not, it was in order to save on rental expenses. It was a definite change.

1974

It was at this time I met with the hardcore reality of Black on Black crime; it was also when I met my first boyfriend. Mom worked at night as a bartender, so I was left to myself most nights. I found myself getting into trouble because no one kept an eye on me. I so desperately wanted love that I began to dress in a provocative manner in order to get attention. I soon discovered it wasn't quite the kind of attention I was looking for.

Like many of the teens in the area, I was a regular up at Centinela Park. One day while riding my 10 speed bike to the park with my new radio wrapped around the handle bars, blaring 1970 hits of the day (it was the kind that was shaped like a gigantic bracelet and could be opened in the middle and worn or hung on an object), I stopped to use the bathroom and left the bike right outside the bathroom opening. When I emerged from the restroom, my bike along with the radio was gone and I was surrounded by a gang of Crips. They seemed to have appeared out of nowhere; in less than a few moments they had covered a large portion of the park. There must have been over one hundred and fifty of them. They were both male and female, and they had camped right outside the bathroom. Once I had fully emerged from the restroom, I noticed one of the guys had taken off on my bike and was circling a small area not far from me. Immediately I was targeted by one of the girls who began accusing me of "eyeing her man," as she put it. Before I could utter a word, I was hit full force in the face - with her fist. The impact from the hit spun me around causing me to stumble and fall to the ground. I laid there in shock for a moment, but quickly gained enough strength to catch a glimpse of my surroundings only to realize that things were about to go from bad to worse. You see gangs traveled in packs almost like wolves, and they could sense my fear escalating as I tried to reason with her about having no interest in her man. This only served to further enrage her, as though I was rejecting him and somehow I had rejected her as well. It was like a feeding frenzy of sharks; it was as though the rest of the girls could smell blood and sensed my fear. One by one, girl after girl... more and more jumped into the fight. Fist upon fist, I was pummeled.

After that, I withdrew for a while and would freak out when too many people were around me. It was shortly after the attack that my mother contacted my father whom she had kept in contact with over the years. Plans for me to visit were soon in the making.

Once I regained a little composure, I became somewhat promiscuous and started experimenting with drugs and alcohol. When I started dating an 18 year old from Compton, a gang-banger who had given me a diamond ring right after graduation, my mom had had enough. That summer I would take my first trip to Chicago to meet my dad for the first time.

My mom had been in touch with him over the years and probably had shared some concerns about my lack of direction and her fear of where my future was heading. A flood of emotions hit me when I realized the man who I had always longed for and wanted desperately to see was about to be face to face with me. It was about a three hour plane ride to Chicago from LA. We would meet for the first time at the O'Hare airport terminal. He stood a staggering six feet six inches tall. Clean shaven with a muscular upper body and smaller waist, his long legs looked like trees. At first it was a little awkward, but he broke the silence with an off-the-wall joke. It was a good feeling knowing there was another person responsible for my being here. Even though I did not understand the issues surrounding their separate lives, I was glad to know I was accepted. As we rode the escalator down to the street level, I noticed I was getting a lot of unwarranted stares...my appetite for attention dismissed it all. It was 1975 in Chicago and mixed heritage was still an oddity. I stayed in a two-bedroom apartment with my father and his sister Barbara. I think I slept on the hide-a-bed couch at the time. The living conditions were cramped at best. I had heard my father had a drinking problem and indulged in a smoke or two. He also had an addiction to pornography.

One morning I wanted to make something in the oven and was told I had to light the broiler in order to cook. As I knelt down to light the broiler, I was thrown back by a rush of gas and flames that singed my hair, removed my eyebrows, and fused my eyelashes together. Luckily, I was not burned at all. We traveled to Harvey Illinois, where I met my two half-sisters Tiki and Toni. That was the beginning of a new life for me and a new found will to not only survive, but to thrive in this life.

When I returned home, my mother wanted to move us back to West Los Angeles/Culver City, but I convinced her to let me go to school with my Jr. High friends. This would mean catching the bus to Westchester every day from Inglewood, or she could drive me there and drop me off. It wasn't long before she grew tired of the commuting.

Chapter 6
High School & The Fast Life

W hen I started 10th grade at Westchester High School, we (the Black community of youth) were met with the full on fury of the upper middle class White beach community over the integration of the Los Angeles county school system. The first day at school, we experienced a hostile crowd of parents from the community armed with baseball bats. Gathered at the back gates of the school they resembled a scene from *Remember the Titans.*

Tensions ran high everywhere. People were running down hallways threating to fight anybody who was not their color. At one point, a Black male student ran up to me and asked me this question without hesitation, "Are you ready to kick some white-a**?." I think my response caught him totally by surprise as I found myself in that same place once again; that place where I had taken a stand once before back at Culver City Junior High School.

I was livid! What was wrong with him? I thought. With clinched fist and an intensity I had never felt before, I glared at him and sternly posed this question, "And what side should I fight on, my mother's or my father's?!" After my anger subsided, I kind of felt sorry for him; He looked as though he had seen a ghost. It was apparent he had never even given thought to the possibility that I was biracial. He couldn't seem to gather himself together after that. I will never forget the puzzled look on his face. Nor will I forget the determination I felt that day to never again allow someone to make me feel in order to be considered legitimate, I would have to choose between cultures or negate my heritage.

I made it through another year and a half at another school when we relocated to West Los Angeles; this time I would attend Alexander Hamilton High School, home of the Hami High Yankees. Man. How I hated starting a new school in the middle of the year, but by now I had mastered the change of venue. The school was about five miles from Venice Beach and close in proximity to Beverly Hills and West Hollywood. It had a very distinct culture, diverse and full of entertainers both in sports and on stage. This is where I would begin the process of coming into myself, or so I thought. It was mid-October when I started. I quickly enrolled in courses I loved most, music and sports.

1976

I joined the gymnastics team first, took drama and signed up for choir. I did really well in these areas which helped tremendously with my GPA, but I had difficulty with study habits, I had none. So, I ditched school and smoked a little marijuana here and there. Once I smoked something lined with

PCP and did the Chinese split (legs out to the side instead of front and back) on the back lawn of the school without any pain whatsoever- I couldn't feel anything.

Thank God for his mercy in my life during this time. At another time, while walking down the hall during a passing period, I was motioned by someone to come over and try sniffing something up my nose. It was a liquid of some sort. I found out later it was heart medication. The rush could have killed me; it caused me to fall halfway down a flight of stairs and resulted in a badly sprained ankle. There was a lot of ditching school and sometimes a bus ride out to Compton or to the beach, whichever suited me at the time.

During my junior year, I met my first real love and lost sight of all else. His name was Patrick and he was a transfer student from Loyola High School. We were together for well over a year, and I was as possessive as anyone could be, almost to the point of obsession. That would end when the choice to abort our child set a forever wedge between us. Depression set in and I spiraled out of control; I shut down while at school and was wheeled off to the nurse's office and sent home.

I found that in crisis my mom was either not at home or sleeping because of working late the night before. This coupled with her nightlife left no time for bonding as a family. The emotional, psychological, and yes, even physical pain in my life had become unbearable. I didn't think I could survive but there it was again, that grace again showing up in my life.

Chapter 7
The Music Industry

I began singing professionally in my senior year of high School. It was just a small group but a welcomed distraction for my traumatized soul, and for a time became my salvation. We did wedding parties, birthday celebrations, and once we sang at Paramount studios for the then T.V. cast of "When Things Were Rotten" (a spoof of Robin Hood and his band of merry men). I taught them all how to do the hustle while on set. As usual, I was the life of the party. Opportunities were beginning to cross my path, for many of them, I was too young and immature to fully appreciate at the time. During my senior year, I blew an audition with Sergio Mendez and his Brazilian Band, Brazil 77 having screamed all night at the Hamilton High Homecoming football game the night before. Without a voice and with a raw throat, it was impossible to perform. I was so angry that I stripped off my form-fitting zip-up coral jumpsuit and plunged right into Sergio Mendez's backyard Olympic sized swimming pool without regard for either the man or his home. I had a lot of nerve back then, but no real respect for people, places or things. The next few years of my life would bring me to the stanch realization that if I wanted to be successful at my craft, that there was going to have to be some major changes. The lifestyle that went with my career choice would soon take its toll.

Me & Derrick

1978

I began making my rounds to all the local club hangouts on Crenshaw strip, then out towards Hollywood and beyond. I was a real road dog and ran the streets with people I didn't even know. I was completely fearless and without a clue to how dangerous the world could be. I even went solo...as long as I could get my party on, I was completely care free.

PART III
Career & Conversion

I visited with friends whose parents lived in Bel-Air mansions and went to Century City Playboy Club parties; all while pursuing my music career. I worked odd jobs; a cashier/clerk for Fotomat, a film developing drop-off booth, a cashier/clerk for Standard Brand Paint Co., and a cashier/sales clerk at a retail clothing store in Los Angeles' famous Fox Hills Mall; all of which were my day jobs. After work, hours were spent at rehearsals and doing demo recordings at various locations such as in-home studios and other designated spots. Still, I found time to enjoy dancing and went out every weekend.

I was a regular at Maverick's Flat night club on Crenshaw Blvd. and was invited to dance on Soul Train by Jeffrey Daniels, one of the main dancers on the television show. While mingling at his birthday celebration, I met James Sylvers who would become my friend and producer for an up and coming group. I would become part of Space Station USA.

Musicians were everywhere in my life. I formed friendships with members of the group *Switch*, whom I had met while dancing on Soul Train. Sounds good, right? What many viewed as a life to be envied was actually covering up a living nightmare.

While seemingly at the pinnacle of success, my mental world was about to explode. You see in between all the glitz and glamour, trauma had occurred time and time again. This was always followed by tremendous mental anguish, but there were the physical anguish traumas as well. Being raised by a single mother was difficult enough but being an only child made me that much more vulnerable. Again, I cannot emphasize enough the mercy of God that was shown to me during this time.

The fact is between the ages of 13-19, I had experienced more pain and abuse than my mind could process. Despite all that I had been able to accomplish; it had left me feeling fatigued and hopeless. The beat down at the public park which left me with a head riddled with lumps, a black eye and stripped down to my bikini bottoms at age 15 had destroyed whatever confidence I had of feeling safe. The two rapes: a gang rape in the projects at 16 which occurred after staying too long at a downtown bus stop and accepting a ride home by strangers and the second at age 19; a home invasion while leaving for work one morning, a total of three abortions and suicide became a real option.

The depression and thoughts of suicide culminated one day in a meltdown in my upstairs bedroom on Plymouth Ave. in Inglewood. I remember it like it was yesterday. It was a fall day in 1978, a somewhat dreary day and I just began to shut down. I was contemplating on how I could take my life and how to do it in the most nonintrusive way. At first, I thought about cutting my wrist, but that would be too bloody I thought. Maybe I could shoot myself but, no guns. So, perhaps jumping out of the large pane window in my room I thought, but what if I survived? After all I might break something and be crippled. Looking back, I can see now that God was using my critical thinking process to reason away the thoughts. Still, I was desperate. I just wanted the pain to go away.

I dropped to my knees and I cried out to God, whoever he was, and asked him to please help me because I just couldn't take any more pain. At that instant, a rush of warmth and peace flooded my soul. The tears streaming down my cheeks all subsided and I sat quietly for hours enjoying an indescribable peace; the bible calls it a peace that passes all understanding. He was real. And he had answered my cry.

From that day on, I was aware of his presence in my life. However; there was always the man trouble. Can't I just find one that makes me happy? All women want somebody good looking that will take care of them, right? What was so hard about that? No matter what anyone thinks, most women want essentially the same thing, an honest and secure relationship with someone who is committed to them and who will provide for and protect them; even if they have the means of providing for themselves.

Chapter 8
Shack'n, Marriage and the Call

I t was 1978 we met at the Century City Playboy Club. They were hosting the Soul Train Awards celebration. The party was jump'n! Everyone was there, Stevie Wonder, Teddy Pendergrass and everyone else in the industry who had a vested interest. I was making my rounds on the dance floor when I realized someone had stolen my purse. Enter tall, dark and all smiles…the man of my dreams. Recognizing a lady in distress, he offered me a ride home because the keys to my mom's Honda were in the purse. I gladly accepted.

Finally, I had found someone who genuinely cared about me. From that day on, we were virtually inseparable. It was a little less than six months into the relationship, when we moved in together. After all, that was long enough to know if you could get along without killing each other, right? We moved into a little one bedroom apartment on West Blvd, right next to his Spirit filled church going mom. I'm sure she was totally ecstatic about the floozy who had moved in with the son whom she had been no doubt praying for. Nevertheless, she tolerated me. She had been trying to get him to go to church with her, but he was enjoying life's sinful pleasures and was not too interested in attending services at the time.

A few months into the relationship, I began to feel conflicted about living together without being married, which was odd because I had seen my mother do it for years. Nevertheless, I could not shake the feeling, so I told the live in boyfriend that we could no longer have relations until we were married.

Well, this is where things got very interesting. It was at this point when I found out about the ex-wife and twins he had left behind. The problem was that he never made sure there was a divorce. Now what? Well something had to be done because I was not going to hang around living in limbo. I pressed him to take care of the paperwork believing this should do the trick, but something just didn't sit right. Hmm? Could it be God was not in agreement with my summation of the situation? After all, what did his Word say about it? Something I would have to ask myself time and time again.

Chapter 9
Disobedience, Children and Divorce

The fact was I heard the Lord say loud and clear go back home to your mother's house. "I don't think so." I said to myself. I'm not going back there to stay with her and her crack-addict boyfriend! You see, for the past six years my mom had been seeing this man and now they were living together. That was one of the reasons for me moving out in the first place. So I told God, *"this is the deal."* I'm willing to negotiate. I'll get him saved, he will get divorce papers, we will get married and we'll stay here. After all, surely he would be pleased with this compromise and should be happy I am at least willing to look like I care about appearances. It was a total of six months before the finalization of the divorce would take place. I'm unsure of how long ago the relationship had ended, and why he never felt the need to make sure it was completely dissolved.

In the meantime, there would be no physical involvement. Once that was taken care of, the next step was to get married. I should have known something when, no one showed up to my bridal shower. God will speak through your circumstances, if you listen. Anyway, we got married at the Justice of the Peace in downtown Inglewood.

For the occasion, not realizing the somberness of the event, I came dressed in a pair of jeans and a black t-shirt that had printed across the front *"My body belongs to me but I share."* I really had no clue as to what marriage was all about; I thought it was just the legal way to have sex. We were married three days before my 21st birthday, on October 21, 1979. Of course neither one of us had the slightest idea of what marriage looked like. His father left while he was young and my parents were unable to marry. We were from two very different worlds except for that common thread.

My mother was White and a preacher's daughter from Muncie, Indiana and his mother was Black from Kansas City, Missouri. Like most African Americans born in the U.S., descendants of slaves, struggling for equality and a place of respect in this country. This is not a judgment on her or anyone else, it's just historical fact.

This would greatly hinder my understanding of how to deal with communicating effectively in the marriage and why we both were so self-absorbed and dysfunctional. As the old saying goes, hindsight is 20/20. I can confidently attest to being able to see things much clearer now.

The Invitation

It was shortly thereafter that his mom, who had repeatedly tried to get him to attend services, invited us to go to church. She was probably quite surprised when I said yes. It may have not been the first invite, maybe not even on the second try, but eventually we both went and that's when it all began. It was a cool morning, she had prepared us the night before. It would be really crowded so we would have to get there by 6:30 am. "Are you kidding me?" I thought to myself.

Who in their right mind gets up before dawn to go to church? When we arrived at the church on Crenshaw Blvd. the line was literally wrapped around the entire building with folks waiting to get in. I thought I was at a club. It took standing in line for an hour and a half before we were able to get inside to sit down. Once seated, I was just a little intimidated. You see, I had no knowledge of church, church clothes or church folks.

At one point I was overwhelmed by the sheer size of the congregation, there were over 1600 in the sanctuary alone and another two or three hundred in the overflow. A sudden fear arose and a knot in the pit of my stomach screamed, "I've got to get out of here!" I rushed out the foyer doors and into the lady's bathroom down the hall. My heart pounding inside my chest, how would I get out of here? There was a phone in the hall. I tried to get someone to pick me up but, no one answered the phone. No one was available to come and get me.

So, after a few minutes of composure, I reluctantly walked back inside and took my seat. I remember the choir singing a few songs and then the minister got up to speak. I cannot recall the message but, I remember being pulled and compelled by the alter call and went forward as requested. I would confess Christ that day publicly; the ushers then escorted us back to a room for prayer and instruction.

As I passed through the door of the prayer room, I noticed some people had their hands up and were weeping out loud and others were speaking in some strange language, almost scared me half to death. I didn't know what to think. The lady ministering to me calmed my fears and explained what was taking place. She then asked if I would like prayer for the infilling of the Holy Spirit, "No that's alright," I said. She handed me a packet of materials to read and off I went.

Later that evening, while in my bedroom at home, I prayed a very simple prayer in my head, "whatever you want me to have God, give it to me," I prayed. There in my room all alone, God filled me with His spirit and with the evidence of speaking in other tongues as the book of Acts makes reference to in Chapter 2. I may have been saved a year prior to this by having given my life to Christ, but this time around there was an impartation. There was a sin overcoming power in my life that God had now given to me in the way of his Holy Spirit. The difference was like comparing a firecracker with a stick of dynamite. I recognized then that it was the enemy of my soul who wanted to steer me away from the answer to all my questions.

Chapter 10
The Breaking

My first test of obedience came in the way of prioritizing my life. The dying to self would not come easy for me; I was a self-centered only child and had done things my way since my youth. I developed a great love for God because he had first loved me and in spite of my messed-up life, I was willing to be broken. It came in the way of first letting go of my career. Up until that time, music was still my main point of focus, My God-if you will. However, two months into the marriage, after my water baptism, I noticed I had been having a queasy feeling and decided to visit the doctor.

I found out that I was pregnant with my first child. That was a turning point in my life. I could no longer see myself up on stage in tight black spandex pants singing about being freaky. The decision to walk away was a difficult one but. While watching Christian television and under the conviction of the Holy Spirit, I heard Nancy Harmon of *The Love Special* say you can't serve two masters. My decision was made. Needless to say, my producer at the time was not very happy and had some choice words for me.

I worked hard at being a wife and a mother, along with trying to navigate through my new found faith. I began reading about how God had supernaturally used people in the Bible, about signs and wonders and the mighty works Christ had done while He was on this earth. I simply took God at his word. I could not get enough of the Word. Soon friends and family grew tired of hearing me preach all the time, but it was like fire shut up in my bones. I would tell everyone I came in contact with about Jesus; at the market, at the bus stop, and anywhere else I could.

I was truly a changed person, just how much so, I would find out while attending my first Christian Concert. Since becoming a Christian, I had gotten rid of all my music and listened to only music centered on Christ. I really wanted nothing more to do with that former life. One day, while listening to Christian radio, the announcer said the next caller would receive a free ticket to hear Roby Duke in concert, and even though I had never heard of him, I was thrilled at having the chance to go to a concert. I picked up the phone and dialed the number. Sure enough, I got through and won the ticket!!!

It was at a small theater but I didn't care. I was excited to go. About halfway into the concert, it was announced there would be a short intermission. As I turned to walk out to the foyer area, I was approached by the emcee who hesitantly asked if my name was Dana. I replied. "Yes." The next question really puzzled me, as it was a Christian concert. "Are you saved?" He asked. "Yes, I am," I replied with a little bit of a snarl, to which he replied, "There is a God!" "Excuse me?" I said, not understanding his response to my answer.

Why would he ask me such a question? Then came the Shock. It turned out that he had once tried to date me back in high school and he told me the last time he saw me, I was in the Fox Hills Mall shoplifting. "You must be mistaken." I said, "I am no thief." I got royally upset about the accusation and stood fast on my conviction that it could not have been me.

It wasn't until the Holy Spirit gently reminded me of what a wretched soul I truly was before Christ came into my life that it dawned on me. "Wow!" What a change had taken place, I thought. I had completely forgotten about that part of my life.

I found myself at every prayer group meeting I could make. This was great. Soon I began to experience a powerful presence of God in my life and He began to tug at my heart and fill me with a compassion for the lost. One Sunday, while attending a class for prayer and praise at Crenshaw, I had an encounter with God that would change everything. While everyone else was praying I felt an overwhelming presence come upon me. The Lord began to speak to me about how He felt about the people and their hearts toward Him. He said they praised him with their lips but their hearts were far from him. The feeling was so intense it felt as if 1000 pounds were sitting on me.

I could sense the Spirit of God wanted me to speak in my unknown tongue louder, above the rest of the people - it scared me. I held out as long as I possibly could before a burst of a few sentences came forth, followed by the English interpretation of what He had revealed to me earlier.

Back to back they came, with a boldness and intensity that seemed different than the other prayer languages. Once the classroom was dismissed, I noticed everyone was staring at me. I soon got a reputation around the church and tried to get in to see the pastor; there was a nine month waiting list. Nothing was in place to address what was happening to me and what to expect with the call upon my life.

Every once in a while, a word of prophesy would come forth at the church, at one service in particular I can remember a choir member bringing forth a powerful word having to do with someone called a servant of God. Little did I know or understand the word was to be for me. As she spoke the words, they seemed to pierce my very being and I began to shake in my seat. I could sense a presence much stronger than my own and knew God was once again dealing with me about the call.

I had begun prophesying and laying hands on people seeing miracles happen and delving into the deep things of God. The only problem was the fruit of the spirit had not caught up with the gifts. That is where true maturity comes in. I had a long journey ahead of me and I was not going to make it easy for

God to teach me. I was growing and thriving, or so I thought, but the toll on my new marriage was evident; poor communication and the lack of interest in each other's life left us both isolated and lonely. Looking back, I can see we were in need of serious mentoring, but we had not availed ourselves to counsel until it was too late.

These were formative years in the body and I experienced the under belly of the ill prepared ministry. I got to see it first hand, up close and personal. Misogyny, prejudice, and a host of other related dysfunctions among believers.

There were too many obstacles to overcome and I was too stubborn to wait it out. I wasn't going to take any more and I wanted out of the trap I felt stuck in. Three and a half years was all I could take. This was not the life I had signed up for. Poverty, marriage, two babies and no breathing room. It was too much for me to handle. After all, I gave up my music career, for what? What more do you want from me? At this time a friend and confidant came along in the form of a young woman from Ohio. She was visiting her aunt in Los Angeles and we became fast friends. We spent many days together sharing the Lord, but I was neglecting my duties as a wife.

Unintentional as it was, it caused jealousy and suspicion in my home. When her aunt kicked her out because of losing her job, we took her in and that made things even worse. One day in a heated argument she was put out. I had enough and out the door I went. This was as unwise a thing to do as getting married in the first place. Hurt and angry, we both avoided each other, and after a short separation another woman moved into our small apartment with a young child claiming it to be his.

I was devastated.

Once again, I had made a mess of things, but that move-in sealed the fate of our relationship. It would be almost a year long struggle to find some direction in my life - living with different people from different countries and no employment. I finally obeyed and went to live with my mother in Perris, California But only after I had lost everything else and had dwindled down to about 98 lbs.

I was just being plain ole' rebellious. If there was one thing I appreciated about God, it was his honest dealings with me. I may not have always been obedient, but I was always honest with him when confronted about my shortcomings. This would help to keep me sane through all the ups and downs in my life and believe me there were many.

Chapter 11
Starting Over

In 1982, I found myself back home with mom and her boyfriend, again. Now what? I really hated to go back home, especially with the cowboy boyfriend, and to live in Perris, California. Had I been obedient in the first place and not gotten married, this is where I would have ended up anyway. It was a little country town about two hours outside of Los Angeles.

The roads were made of dirt and the street signs were white wooden posts stuck near the fork in the roads - just wooden stakes. Which by the way could barely be seen at night. The only visible lights at night came from the shopping center downtown. Man, this was a far cry from the busy streets of Los Angeles. My kids were only two and three years old then. I was still completely clueless as to what God wanted me to do with my life.

Not long after I moved in with my mom and Tony, the live-in boyfriend of eight years, I was washing clothes at the local laundry mat, when I was greeted by a tall man with a big grin. I'll never forget Brother Myers. He invited me to church as he was one of the ministers at Riverside Faith Temple. The joy of the Lord oozed out of his very being. His wife Renee was a hair dresser in Perris, and I have yet to find anyone who does their craft as well as she.

Up until then, I was wasting my life hanging out across the street at the Old West Saloon playing pool and listening to the jukebox. Some days I worked out with Jane Fonda and other workout videos trying to keep my girlish figure. Every once in a while I would go roller skating out in Riverside. Life was very simple and to a city girl, like me, very boring.

I had found one friend though; she was the daughter of the bar tender at the Old West. Her name was Tyra, she too was biracial, only her mom was Black and dad was White. We both ended up at the church in Riverside - after I encouraged her to go. It seemed like my mom and her boyfriend Tony knew everyone in Perris and despite my lack of respect for the man, I could still acknowledge what a gifted individual he was. He could make something out of almost anything. For instance, he could make leather belts decorated with silver and jewelry from eating utensils and turquoise. He even made dog houses from old discarded telephone spools for their Doberman Pinchers.

We just never hit it off very well, and I did everything in my power to stay clear of him. I would come up with things to do in order to get out of the house. Although I was never really a fan of education, I decided to go back and finish high school. I was only one class short of the requirements for graduation. It wasn't important to me while I was pursuing the music career; after all I was going to be a *"DIVA!"*

Now, here I was on welfare and food stamps living with mom and Ole crack head. I had a serious attitude problem. Who was I to sit around judging anybody? But, when you are immature and selfish, that's what you do. I didn't know his story, or what had taken place in his life to cause enough pain that he had to deaden it with such a strong toxin. But, no matter what I thought about his problems or assumed about his life, I had no room for judgment. I needed to get my own life in order.

Chapter 12
School and Unknown Potential

I took the dare. I finished my diploma requirements and headed off to Jr. College. A new found friend in Perris had recognized I did not see my own potential and encouraged me to further my education. "I don't think so," I said. I have a calling on my life to preach and don't see any reason to detour from that call; I was quite emphatic about that. After all, surely God did not want me to waste my time with a bunch of non-believing eggheads. You couldn't tell me anything about God in college.

I was about to find out God has his way of getting you to your destiny, even when you don't understand it. In every one of my transitional periods, He proved He was more than enough God to bring me to a place of understanding…His way of developing a disciple.

The Lord began prodding me and pricking my heart concerning the enrollment process. Of course I was totally uninterested until He whispered quietly to my heart telling me there were souls on campus that needed to be reached. He had to appeal to the evangelist in me in order to motivate me in their direction.

At this time, I had already joined Riverside Faith Temple Church. I began attending Riverside Community College in 1985. I joined the choir and the young adult ministry and even began attending minister's class acknowledging the call God had placed on my life. I seemed to be doing pretty well. Other than the trouble I would occasionally get into by prophesying outside of the church i.e. RCC Mass choir concerts, Campus Crusade for Christ and anywhere else I could manage.

I am sure I embarrassed my pastor on more than one occasion. However, Pastor Sims was quite a patient man. Still, all and all, things were pretty good. I had good friends and lots of fellowship, but I was broke. On one particular Sunday a visiting church came through as I was leading the Hallelujah chorus. Afterwards, I was approached by the visiting minister about coming to sing at their fellowship.

I jumped at the chance, "great" I thought. It would be a grievous error on my part and would take many years of recuperation to get back to the maturation process for the call of God on my life. Thank God for the promise of working all things together for the good in the life of a believer. How He does it, is a mystery, but He does all things well. The lure of a bigger and seemingly upwardly mobile church was just too good to pass up, so out the door I went. Just call it being a silly woman, enough said.

I sang and everyone loved it. I stayed and joined the choir, but the standard was very different than the safety I had known back at Faith Temple. Things were going on I had no knowledge of, nor understanding about military life. I was a naïve baby Christian who thought more highly of herself than she ought.

I was introduced to a very handsome man at the church, who was very impressed with my gift and asked me out. The pastor suggested it was a good thing. It turned out he was a married man. Although they were separated, the principle of the word was still very clear. Needless to say, good looks and a million dollar smile was all it took. I fell for him hook line and sinker.

He was older than me by 16 years and apparently had an eye for the ladies. I was caught like a deer in the headlights. Should have stayed put and stayed with the Word, but as so many women do, I went with the female tendencies of emotional reasoning. Unfortunately for me, it would not be the last time. Now I don't broach this subject lightly, I am well aware of the entrapments of the enemy and the snares placed in the lives of single women, especially single mothers. I am writing this in order to help expose the lies of the enemy concerning women and to help steer them clear of his deception.

This decision resulted in me becoming a single parent of three now, instead of two. It set me back concerning my goals, attending school and the ministry. More than anything, it was a very painful experience. I finally left the church after being humiliated at his having left the ministry and leaving me to face the ridicule alone. Where was the compassionate counsel - anybody? Afterwards, I returned to live once more with mom, this time in a single-wide trailer; she and Tony had split up. Back to Perris, complete with live-in dogs and cats and in the middle of what looked like a desert. It did not take long for me to get the hint I was going to have to change if I was ever going to find a better life for myself. I had several roommates over the years and tried it one more time, just to move out from my mom's place. This time it would be a move to a Moreno Valley subculture, Edgemont.

This was a particularly rough side of town, but it was all that we could afford. I moved in with my friend Cindy, until I could afford to move into my own apartment. I joined a local church because it was more economical for me rather than going all the way into Riverside, that reasoning too would cost me later on. I lived below the poverty-line for several years. This kept me in the roughest part of town; Republic Ave. Near Alessandro and Ellsworth, an area with such a bad reputation they have since changed the names of the adjacent streets. I lived there for three years and in that time; I walked the streets preaching to anyone that would stand still long enough to hear the message. I saw drug dealers saved, children give their lives to Christ, a man died after not heeding a word from the Lord, and the miraculous healing of a sparrow.

All this while I was broke and on state-aid. There are vivid memories of that place and I learned a lot during those years. Things that would be the foundation on which a future ministry would be built. There I obtained much needed wisdom about people, the vulnerability of being a single mother and about being a little too naïve about the nature of men. When there is no male representation in the home, children suffer from a lack of affirmation and a feeling of insecurity.

It was also at this time I allowed a young man to stay in my home that had no place to live; little did I know that rebellion had been the reason for his condition in the first place. Unfortunately, anytime a person refuses to take counsel for their own good, they inevitably learn the hard way that this is in fact a consequence. I told him he had to go because he refused to honor the established curfew. He ended up in jail and gave my address to an inmate. That inmate became my pen pal for two and a half years; this too was a poor decision. As I look back now, it is very clear to me my poor reasoning concerning men had much to do with the fact there was no father in the home to affirm, protect, or provide for me. Something that used to plague the Black community, but has since spread throughout the nation and is now an epidemic.

Whoops, I did it again! Didn't wait on the Lord

How in the world did I get here? It felt safe just writing to someone incarcerated; after all he had changed and had given his life to the Lord, right? Ladies beware. There is a reason the brother went to jail in the first place. Far too often, there is a lack of accountability among believers in the body of Christ and this often causes babes in Christ to become susceptible to many of the entrapments of the enemy. In all you are getting, get an understanding. A woman without a covering will always make a good target for the enemy and there are many today. Wisdom was not the primary concern for me at this time and I paid dearly for it.

Here we go again with baby number four, after which I was totally spent. (Slang for had nothing left to give). I had gotten tired of repenting to God for all of the short comings in my life, but His love for me kept me coming back time and time again. You see the main problem with we humans is our inability in recognizing that we are all imperfect and need a savior bigger than ourselves; our philosophies and our own vain imagination.

We compare ourselves with one another, or judge ourselves by ourselves and always coming up short. We need to view ourselves and our value systems, philosophies, and beliefs by the scrutiny of his word. I never thought I would ever be able to recuperate from the trauma, but as the scripture declares, *"I can do all things through Christ which strengthens me!"* So, once more I squared those shoulders, picked up my cross and kept moving and pressing towards the mark. It was extremely difficult at times, but God never gave up on me. I learned firsthand, that He was in fact a miracle worker.

Chapter 13
Restoration

I learned God does in fact give second chances, and in my case so much more. After the loss of my job at the bank, I stayed home with the last little one until he was old enough to be left with a babysitter so I could return to school. I learned some truly difficult lessons through all of this, but I was determined God would somehow get the glory from even my biggest mess-ups.

Over the next few years, I began to discover some very interesting family endowments on either side of my family. While at a family reunion on my mother's side, my maternal grandmother handed me a book written by and about a distant relative. It was a book about my great-great-great grandmother, Maria Woodworth-Etter. At the time, I had recently given birth to my forth child and really didn't pay it much attention. I felt no real connection to my mother's side of the family and everyone seemed to be more comfortable having it that way. If I weren't around, then neither would the awkward feelings that arose at my presence be either. At least that is the way it felt for most of my life. Of course, I can only speak from my personal view. I cannot judge the actions of my mother's family, other than to say love is greater than any amount of fear. To the onlooker and to any psychologist worth his salt, it could be ascertained I was in serious need of therapy.

How fortunate I was to have found the wonderful counselor himself. Jesus! After the passing of both parents, my dad in 2006 and my mom in 2012, I began the arduous task of reconnecting to both sides of my family. To date, the healing process has produced relationships with brothers, sisters, aunts, uncles, cousins, nieces and nephews that span from the East to the West coast. The untold story of a rich heritage across three very distinct cultures, African American, European and Native American. Most importantly: I have acquired a deep compassion for others and an even richer heritage in mercy and grace.

Maria and daughter Elizabeth

Great grandfather Earl Clark Sr. Beulah and children

Grandfather Earl Clark Jr. and Jesse & kids

My Maternal Side

Maria Woodworth-Etter: *The Great Evangelist.*

She is known as the grandmother of the Pentecostal movement here in the United States and is listed in Who's Who among Religious Leaders in America. But those familiar with her simply called her Sister Etter; with only a third grade education, she would become one of the most profound preachers of her day traveling over 13,000 miles and holding tent meetings with attendance in the thousands. In fact, she was almost jailed for not segregating her meetings and openly welcomed and accepted both the African American and Native American communities.

She had a passionate desire for education but had to work in the mills in order to help provide for the siblings in her family. After the sudden death of her father due to heat stroke, she worked diligently to help as long as she possibly could. She would ultimately answer God's call upon her life. She married at first for purposes of securing a respectful place in society; women were not permitted to preach at the time. Security and acceptance meant everything for the women of her day. Unfortunately, the marriage would end with his having had an affair followed by a subsequent divorce. She would marry a second time for ministry. She had six children and lost all but one to childhood diseases. Lizzie would be the sole survivor and the grandmother of my grandfather Earl Woodrow Clark. To this day the church founded by Maria is still standing and staffed. Although the name has been changed it still remains at its original location in Indianapolis Indiana.

My Paternal side photo on the next page

My great-great grandmother Annie wearing a black hat is seated at the table. My great grandparents, Mr. & Mrs. John Solomon Clinton Dewitt Lyons are found in the center of the photo, my grandmother Helen is standing to their right and my father is the little boy seated on my great aunt's lap at the table. (Taken 1940's)

The Lyon's family, my dad's mother's family

One of the most respected organists in Indiana, she played for Billy Graham Crusades and for Martin Luther King Jr's funeral at the Kennedy Center. Her family was originally from the Tennessee territory and part of Church of God in Christ. Her sister, Missionary/Evangelist Elisabeth Moore was secretary to Mattie Moss Clark. My grandmother married and moved to Muncie where she was abandoned by her first husband (my father's father) and married a second time. A little over a generation removed from slavery, my aunt shared with me her difficulty in reconciling the fact she had a granddaughter perceived to be part of the oppressor and the fact her son fathered a mixed child by a White woman.

Mamie Carter, my dad's father's mother

Helen's family originated in Knoxville, Tennessee and was part of the black-side of Pentecost in America; Whereas, most of dad's family had roots in Georgia. Many people know nothing about the Azusa Street Revival which took place in Los Angeles, California or the split in the movement down the color line. It is a very interesting study in our history. Helen is the mother of my father, James Edward Carter (now deceased) and my aunt Barbara. Her life too was racked by pain and prejudice, but I believe she gained great solace through her musical gifting. Getting to know my father's side of the family after meeting him at 16 and the two subsequent meetings that followed were enlightening. It remains an ongoing process. And although I would only get the chance to visit him once more before his death, I have had the pleasure of meeting many of my relatives and reconnecting with both the maternal and paternal sides of my family. Mamie, my father's grandmother, had ten children and I have recently become acquainted with their descendants thanks to social media.

It has been said the most segregated time of the week is on Sunday morning. Even today after the civil rights movement, cultural exchanges, relativism, multicultural competency, sensitivity training and the likes, we are still in denial. Slavery and its residuals are still being felt. I find it intriguing, that I have been able to trace my mother's side of the family all the way back to the 14th century and can only trace my father's back to the 1800's (and that's sketchy at best), but it points to the inequity which has existed for generations. In either case, the men in our family seem to be somewhat absent down through the years; that headship being a very crucial part of family dynamics.

My maternal grandfather, Sister Etters's great grandson, is depicted with his parents Earl Clark Sr. and Beulah Clark and his younger sister. According to my mother's recollection, He did not show much in the way of affection towards his children. A sentiment confirmed by her siblings as well. There were the girls, Mary and Earlene (my mom) and three boys, David, Earl, (my mom's twin) and the youngest Charles. I grew up with little interaction with her side of the family and since I did not have any relations with my father's side until later in my adult years, men for the most part had no significant role in my young life.

As I look back, I can see that every failed relationship can be reflective of not only my lack of knowledge concerning the way in which men thought, but due in large part to their own struggles and issues with identity problems. Each one had a story that depicted either an negligent abusive or absent father. A very real dysfunction within our society, especially among Black males due to the residuals of slavery. Having done my undergraduate work in African/African American Studies along with my degree in Human Relations and subsequent counseling experience, I have gained a great deal of understanding, not only of my family dynamics, but that of urban communities in general.

I am ever learning about the social dynamics that lay at the base of so many relationships and hope that what I have learned through both my personal and educational experience will help to bridge the gap for others to come. My prayer is for reconciliation at large and that the world would know us by our love one for another; and that all people are created by God. We did not choose who our parents would be or the location of our birth, but we can choose how we interact with one another and the people whom we share this world with. It will take some time and effort on our part to get to know our neighbor, but it will be well worth the effort especially in the days ahead of us.

We should be encouraged in knowing this verse applies to us all.

"I will praise thee; for I am fearfully and wonderfully made: marvelous are thy works; and that my soul knows right well," (Psalm 139:14).

Chapter 14
Indiana History

Th here is quite a bit of historical information here that bears
mentioning in order to understand both time frames
referenced as well as context. The two migration periods which
took place among the Black population between my birth and
that of my mother's brought profound changes in American
society at the time. Although this is not an academic book, I
would be remiss, if I did not provide some very crucial
information for clarification and to educate those who would
otherwise not garner an understanding of its historical value.

Indiana Midpoint for the Underground Railroad

There was such a striking difference between the life of my
father and that of my mother. Had it not been for the
coursework received while earning my undergraduate degree in
African/African American Studies, I would never have
understood how great the existing gulf really was. The
Underground Railroad ran right through the middle of Indiana.
It was a system used by slaves in order to escape their
deplorable condition. The system of going from safe place to
safe place provided by individual families, many of those
families were White who would at their own peril house
runaway slaves in pursuit of their freedom, allowing many to
start a new life. It seems absurd in today's culture of political
correctness that this was a reality in our not so distant past. But
this is our this nation's history and we need to own it, address it
and repent of it. Institutionalized racism was a way of life, and
is still an acceptable practice in certain parts within our society.
To be perfectly honest, I had to really pray my way through the

information that I received, it was both disturbing and at the same time inspiring. But in the end, it would fuel my desire for racial reconciliation.

Indiana and the Ku Klux Klan

By 1922 the state had the largest KKK organization nationally. It averaged 2,000 new members per week from July 1922 to July 1923. Indiana's Klan organization reached its peak of power in the following years, when it had 250,000 members, an estimated 30% of native-born white men. By 1925 over half the elected members of the Indiana General Assembly, the Governor of Indiana, and many other high-ranking officials in local and state government were members of the Klan. (Wikipedia) Politicians had also learned they needed Klan endorsement to win office, this was considered to be a stronghold for racists (a fortified place).

It is apparent to me now as I am older, that God indeed had a plan for my life and reveals more and more of that plan as I mature as a believer.

Middletown USA

Many people are unaware of the interest that Muncie, Indiana held for researchers; one in particular was the ISRR, Institute for Social and Religious Research. To grasp how Muncie became a barometer of American life requires an understanding of the origins of the first Middletown research. The Lynds were executing a "small city study" commissioned by the (ISRR). Launched with the financial support of oil magnate John D. Rockefeller, Jr., the ISRR sought religious solutions to the social problems of industrial America. Rockefeller was alarmed by escalating class conflict in the early twentieth century. He believed religious activism offered the most likely means of reducing the tensions of industrial life and so funded the organization that would become ISRR. As for the growing Black population they simply ignored it, making "Middletown" a whiter community than 1920s Muncie. (Wikipedia)

There is another study aptly named *The Other Side of Middletown* which takes a look at the Black community during the same time period. The project takes a more realistic view of the racial dynamics that made up the town's diverse community.

I may have missed out on the closeness of family ties throughout my younger years, but God has more than blessed me in subsequent years. In this past decade, I have been afforded the rare opportunity of using my gift of song in laying to rest, four of my precious loved ones, my grandparents Earl and Jesse Clark and my parents James Carter and Earlene Clark. It is a joy knowing I will see them all again one day.

As for me, I have learned a great deal from this journey. I have learned about our national heritage, our country's history and about humanity in the broadest sense of the term. Most of all, I have discovered the healing power of forgiveness and the process that makes reconciliation possible. I have been personally aided in many ways; which provided much in the way of insight concerning the why's and how's of human relations as they pertain to racial identity. Furthermore; the acceptance of others as intrinsically valuable has allowed for the restoration of countless relationships including parents and children, siblings and in-laws, as well as the continuation of work with other organizations in facilitating healthy race relations. I have truly found my purpose.

My Wonderful Parents James & Earlene
1957 High School Photographs

1991, Muncie
The first time my parents saw each other after 30 years.

Conclusion

M any things have changed over the years. According to government statistics, by the year 2050 over 50% of the population in America will consist of those born of two or more racial and or ethnic mixes. As nation, we need to be ready, It should be understood by now, that there may be many ethnic groups in this world, but only one race...Human!

**For Speaking Engagements or More Information,
Contact Dana L. Jackson.**

Norman/OKC, OK area

LIFE SOLUTIONS OF NORMAN
Dana L. Jackson
Life Skills Coach/Consultant

Phone: 405-626-1270
Email: highbeam241@gmail.com
http://www.dcjbooks.com

References

Connolly, J. J. (2005). The Legacies of Middletown: Indiana Magazine of History, 101(3), 211-225.

Jackson, Dana. Black by Experience: Poem (2010).

Leonard J. Moore, Citizen Klansmen: The Ku Klux Klan in Indiana, 1921-1928, Chapel Hill: University of North Carolina Press, 1997

Robert S. Lynd and Helen Merrell Lynd, Middletown: A Study in Modern American Culture (New York, 1929).9,

CPSIA information can be obtained
at www.ICGtesting.com
Printed in the USA
LVHW050431180920
666258LV00005B/159

9 781633 020511